Hunger

Hunger

Elise Blackwell

WILLIAM HEINEMANN : LONDON

Published in the United Kingdom in 2003 by William Heinemann

1 3 5 7 9 10 8 6 4 2

Copyright © 2003 by Elise Blackwell

Elise Blackwell has asserted her right under the Copyright, Designs
and Patents Act, 1988 to be identified as the author of this work

William Heinemann
The Random House Group Limited
20 Vauxhall Bridge Road, London, SW1V 2SA

Random House Australia (Pty) Limited
20 Alfred Street, Milsons Point, Sydney
New South Wales 2061, Australia

Random House New Zealand Limited
18 Poland Road, Glenfield
Auckland 10, New Zealand

Random House (Pty) Limited
Endulini, 5A Jubilee Road, Parktown 2193, South Africa

The Random House Group Limited Reg. No. 954009

www.randomhouse.co.uk

A CIP catalogue record for this book
is available from the British Library

Papers used by Random House are natural, recyclable products made
from wood grown in sustainable forests. The manufacturing processes
conform to the environmental regulations of the country of origin

ISBN 0 434 01176 2

Typeset by SX Composing DTP, Rayleigh, Essex
Printed and bound in Great Britain by
Mackays of Chatham plc, Chatham, Kent

For David
and Esme

"We were aware that the visible earth is made of ashes, and that ashes signify something. Through the obscure depths of history we could make out the phantoms of great ships laden with riches and intellect; we could not count them. But the disasters that had sent them down were, after all, none of our affair.

Elam, Nineveh, Babylon were but beautiful vague names, and the total ruin of those worlds had as little significance for us as their very existence. But France, England, Russia . . . these too would be beautiful names . . . And we see now that the abyss of history is deep enough to hold us all."

– Paul Valéry

"You may have noticed the bush that it pushes to air, Comical-delicate, sometimes with second-rate flowers. Awkward and milky and beautiful only to hunger."

– Richard Wilbur, from "Potato"

Hunger

The celebrated biologist Nikolai Vavilov collected hundreds of thousands of seed and plant specimens from around the world, housing them at the Research Institute of Plant Industry in Leningrad. Vavilov became a victim of the antigenetics campaign waged by Trofim Lysenko, who gradually gained control of Soviet agriculture under Stalin. Vavilov died in prison in 1942 or 1943 of some combination of mal-treatment and starvation. Many of his associates and staff were imprisoned, exiled, sent to work on collective farms, or dismissed. During the siege of Leningrad, those who remained protected Vavilov's collections from rats, from human intruders, and from themselves. What follows is a fictional account of such a time and place. The characters are inventions and are in no way based on the courageous people who worked at what today is called the Vavilov Institute.

It is not so uncommon for those near the end of their lives to run their mind's hand over the contours of those lives. Perhaps that is all that I do here as I reach across the populated spaces of time, geography, and language, reach from a comfortable New York apartment to a city once and again called Saint Petersburg.

—

The anniversary of our wedding day fell on the last of the early summer's white nights, and I could still believe that we would be fine. We dined at a restaurant that had been better a few years earlier but was still very good. Our window overlooked the Neva. The Peter and Paul Fortress lifted from the center of the river. Its bastion tilted slightly over the water, seeming more precarious than fortified, pointing askew to a sky more bright than light, a sky the creamy white color of the anona tree's sweet custard apple.

Alena's voice floated lighter on the air than it had in a year, and we ate well, sucking the delicate saltiness from the leg casings of huge crabs, spooning caviar directly into our mouths and sliding it down our throats with a white-grape wine that was just too sweet but good nonetheless.

I kept the check from Alena. She believed that the loss of her salary and the approach of Hitlerite Germany's young soldiers meant that we should hold tight to our money. Like the smell of rain before drops hit the skin, the coming war told me to spend, to have whatever

I could now, before it could no longer be had. It would be later that I would learn to hoard crumbs like a miser.

I desired to go straight home and make love to the only woman I was allowing myself, the only one I really wanted. But Alena had heard on the radio the poet Vera Inber, whose account of the long days and nights ahead would secure her fame and favor, and wished to attend a reading she was giving.

We walked along Nevsky Prospect, which had widened with the crowds out to enjoy the last night of the year when the sun would go to the horizon but no lower. I held Alena close, by her arm, and then closer, by arm around her waist.

Every fabricated thing in Leningrad, from the antique ornaments atop monument gates to the nouveau wire poles, pointed upward, elegant, futile.

The small hall where the reading was held was full and very hot and smoky, something I would savor often in memory but did not enjoy at the time.

I remember few of Vera Inber's words. But those of the reputationless poet who preceded her have remained long with me. Tall and sturdy, he had been a sailor before he seized a pen. He appeared hale on first glance, but the gray folded into his face and the depth and yellow of his eyes gave away some disease of the internal organs.

He read several poems, none of them particularly to my taste, in a strong voice that was decidedly more naval than poetic. The last is the one I remember. It was called "The Ship-wreck Survivor." I offer it now to begin my own story.

I never saw the poem on paper, so I do not know how the sailor-turned-poet broke his lines. But I recall each word as spoken:

"The ones who drown never change the facts, but those who survive the sea in their lungs must send their stories on words, words like small leaky boats, across the distance, cold, and currents of that water."

—

The volunteers of the *opolchenia*, including my Alena but not myself, scurried like rodents. Shelters appeared, and trenches. Young women pierced their skin wrapping barbed wire around obstacles built to prevent tanks from penetrating the city. We all waited for the attack and prepared to defend our city block by block, building by building, hand to hand.

But the tanks never rolled in. They stopped outside the city, and how much simpler it would have been had they kept coming.

—

In early September, the first Hitlerite shells descended – graceful and even hesitant from their high loft. Then Junkers rose and fell, rose and fell, leaving behind deposits of incendiaries like so much fatal silt.

When they hit the Badayev warehouses, the cramped lines of wooden buildings burned fast, and the fats stored within their boards radiated red heat, turning the close sky to embers and filling the air like summer cooking.

What did not burn were a few thousand tons of sugar, which instead melted through the floor planks to survive, shaped and imprinted by the cellars, as a hard candy. This candy was broken into chips that would be prized and sold for money and sex in the months that followed.

But so much would be passed off and paid for as food.

—

Among the many thousands of specimens housed at the institute were several hundred tubers. Small and large. Smooth and warty. White, brown, yellow, purple, and blue. Lidia, my longtime sometimes lover, had helped collect the blue potatoes on an expedition to Ecuador and Peru. I had, against my preference, stayed in Leningrad with Alena.

Lidia collected more than the institute needed, and when she returned, we spent an afternoon in her apartment, peeling, cutting, frying, and feeding the blue chips to each other, licking salt and oil from each other's fingers and the corners of each other's mouths.

Among its many fine qualities, in addition to its deeply earthy taste and sublime color, that particular species of Peruvian blue potato is resistant to the potato blight that starved a million Irish men, women, and children.

—

Heat was gone by the end of September, and all the pipes in Leningrad froze. Until the snow came, we had for washing only muddy Neva water, carried by hand in pail.

—

When we made the decision not to eat the obvious, it was not made all at once but by something like attrition. But it was formalized at a particular moment of a particular day. Before that, we could have still backed away, allowed our unofficial resolve to erode.

Efrosinia was known well throughout the institute only for her brilliance. I could not have told you if she was married or single, where she had been born, nor how she spent her leisure. She was a woman of few extraneous words.

Only one had I seen her verbally agitated – happily so, over research results that were better than she had dared to hope. She had reported them to me rapidly, even breathlessly. When she stopped speaking, it was abrupt. She tucked some loose hair behind her ear, looked up at me from that cut angle, turned, and walked away. It was the only time I had seen her speak unnecessarily.

Some months later, when the findings that had so animated Efrosinia appeared in the very best international journal and caused a stir across the Atlantic, she said nothing but acknowledged our congratulations with only a nod.

So it was surprising, to say the least, that she called a meeting – invited everyone. She invited those of us who had been at the institute with the great director, and she invited the horrid blend of libelers, quacks, opportunists, and mere quietists who had come in since.

And everyone came, nearly filling our large conference room. Efrosinia said what we had been saying tentatively to one another. "We will not eat from the collections, then. We will protect them at all cost."

Efrosinia spoke no more that day. It was others who debated, though the debate was less than I might have thought, less than I might have wanted. Perhaps I wished for a loud din of opposing voices in which to conceal my meek objections to the noble plan. I said nothing.

My Alena spoke briefly in favor of the plan. Vitalii spoke elegantly and – the only one to do so – at length. Even then we all knew that he would be the first to die.

It was not that he was the smallest or weakest. Indeed he was tall and as hardened off as a plant that had never known the indoors. He had been an alpine skier of some renown and had taken an Olympic medal and other awards during the 1920s. He still had the great, wide shoulders, and now, in middle age, plenty of extra pounds around his once athletic waist.

We knew that Vitalii would be the first to die – not, as I have said, because he was the slightest or most vulnerable, not because he had the fewest stores. We knew because it was plain on his face, as plain as the square outside in the bright winter sun on one of Leningrad's thirty-five cloudless days, plain for all but him to see.

Would he have been so brave and clear in our deliberations, the staunchest advocate of martyrdom, our standard bearer, had he known he would not only die but die first of all? No, I believed then and believe even now.

But Vitalii and Efrosinia and, yes, my Alena, carried that day.

—

Forty days into the nine hundred, scientists from our institute and from others braved German fire to pull tubers from the ground of the experimental fields that lay just outside the city's reach. As the count of days rose into the hundreds and was dropped altogether by everyone but historians and masochists, botanists moved to the city's defense. They analyzed land camouflage, carefully – but with strained eyes and stiff fingers – reading over serial air photos of woodland, tundra, bog. They cultivated mushroom spawn, developed collecting and processing methods to render antiseptics from sphagnum. They hunted for new sources of vitamins and medicine. Through their work, they expanded the very definition of edible.

Part of our collection was taken to an

experimental station in Estonia in a convoy of twenty trucks – a move that I helped to plan but was unable, at only the last moment, to join. Those who were able to go posed as Soviet peasants seeking war profits by selling grain to the Hitlerite soldiers. At the Estonian station, Leppik, one of the great director's esteemed colleagues, cared for the seeds for two years. The collection that was under his protection was seized by the German Army late in the war. But it was, quite miraculously, eventually returned intact.

—

I see that it could occur to someone that I am a coward. Maybe I am a coward and maybe I am not. It is not something that matters much to me.

But I would like it to be known that I have also been a brave man. The great director and I had many adventures. We crossed Afghanistan's mountain region of Kafiristan without maps and with only a schoolboy and his old grand-father as guides. It was me, and not the great director, who was bitten by a cobra and took his own knife to his leg. I was the pilot when we had to put down in the Saharan desert and spend the night amid crazed hyenas. We should have stripped off our packs and run when a landslide of rocks and boulders came down on us in the Caucasus, but instead we held our packs and our ground – all to save a few specimens of rare apple. We survived the ridicule and bullets of bandits that overtook us when we were collecting sorghum in Eritrea, and we outsmiled hostiles up and down the Orinoco.

Never did I flinch nor give a thought to running away. Never did I leave a trip early nor decline to enroll at the top of the list for the next. Throughout the institute people commented on my courage.

So maybe I am a coward and maybe I am not, but I am also a brave man. Brave of body and weak of mind, perhaps, lacking in my Alena's long-term, determined moral bravery or the great director's intellectual courage.

If I wished to draw a conclusion, the conclusion I would arrive at is this: if I am a coward, then what I fear are my own thoughts. And my own thoughts were precisely what cold and hunger delivered to me. Brave of body and weak of mind, yes, and alive to think about it.

—

There were many women before Alena, of course. Neighbor girls when I was a boy and then students, waitresses, women I met on the street, on trains, on boats. I would joke, though only to myself, about the perils of transportation.

Most of these women I knew only briefly. A few I loved and stuck with for a time. But I always met the next one.

I thought I could give them all up when I met my Alena. She was kind and cool to me from the start, and I watched her furtively, watched her working harder, earlier, later than everyone else. Small and clear and even, with pleasant features spread neatly, economically, across her face – certainly pretty, but not, upon a single look, remarkably so.

But if you let your eyes linger, let them follow her gaze through her long, straight eyelashes, let them settle on her fine hands as they prepared glass slides and readied the microscope, let your eyes see her bite her lip when perplexed by something she saw but you did not, let yourself watch the bitten lip redden and slightly swell – then you saw a beautiful woman.

I prepared Alena for weeks and weeks, trying to speak to her a bit more – and more personally – every few days, but then sometimes walking past her without comment, a studied neglect that she did not seem to notice. I borrowed a book, loaned her an umbrella. I joined her when I saw her drinking a cup of tea outside on a warm day. I invited her to have lunch with me, to attend an outdoor concert, offered to cook a large dinner for her and then offered again.

But each time she said she was unable to go. Never did she give a reason. It was always and only "I am unable to go."

I continued to see other women, to spend nights with one or two of them. But more and more I thought of only Alena. And always when I thought of Alena, I pictured the Alena who worked and studied and worked more.

Then one day, completely out of the blue, as Americans like to say, she asked me to go with her to the new park of culture and rest just outside the city.

It was styled after Moscow's famous Gorky Park. A few years earlier, I had taken a young woman to Gorky Park's first nighttime carnival, held to celebrate Constitution Day.

Everyone had worn costumes. There were Onegins in green and Tatianas in purple, a black-and-white Charlie Chaplin. I had gone as Mark Antony, and my girlfriend – a tall and stunning brunette – as a beautiful Cleopatra.

I remember the slogan-shouting. A woman dressed as Gorky's mother yelled, "Make fun of those who fall behind!" Someone else screamed, "He who does not laugh, does not eat!"

But there was very little laughter, and I chuckled the next day when the great director showed me a write-up of the Gorky Park carnival in a foreign newspaper. The astute journalist had commented that Russians enjoy themselves without smiling, always taking their pleasure sadly.

Alena and I walked under the park's welcoming banner, LIFE HAS BECOME BETTER, LIFE HAS BECOME MORE CHEERFUL, and took a map of the park's attractions. I remember well how Alena's pale-blue shirt felt ethereally light and silky against my bare arm as we rode the Ferris wheel, how she bowled so much better than I did but never celebrated her victories. I remember thinking that Alena, like those carnival-going Russians that the foreign journalist had poked fun of, took her pleasure sadly.

And I remember thinking that it was a beautiful way to take pleasure, that she did things the right way, the way that I should. I remember almost all of the day that I fell in love with my wife. I remembered it the next day and remember it still.

Yet I did forget, until much later, about the parachute tower. I wanted to jump and Alena did not, and so I teased her about being afraid. But then I saw that it was not fear but something else altogether behind her reticence.

"We've done so many frivolous things today," she said. "I'm at the end of my capacity for it."

She must have been falling in love with me by then, though, because when I asked her to jump anyway, she consented. My wife never refused me, though I could not then and cannot now tell you why. She jumped, seemingly without fear or joy.

I jumped with great fear and great joy.

Later, we watched the dance floor from our table in the beer garden and sipped good lager and snacked on sharp Swiss cheese and spicy sausages. It took all of my self-control not to lick the froth left by the beer on the perfect little curl of Alena's upper lip.

She said, "People court danger to lose themselves or find themselves. Which one do you pursue?"

I looked at this woman I now loved and decided to always tell her the truth. "I don't know. Both, I think."

She nodded, accepting my paltry answer to her good and important question. "I don't need to do either," she said. "I hope that's all right with you."

We married a few months later, and my commitment to be honest and faithful to my strong, perfect wife lasted for more than a year.

—

Sunk by Lysenko before we recognized it, the perils of underestimation. Who could have known that he could market his vernalization – the great director called it *infernalization* – so well to Commissar Yakovlev that the bureaucrat would advocate a Department of Vernalization? But Lysenko was underestimated by many, and the great director was always one to easily dismiss idiotic ideas.

Yet Stalin himself sat in the audience and clapped with his big hands for Lysenko's 1935 speech to the Second All-Union Congress of Shock Collective Farmers – flaming arrows of words that all but named the great director as a class enemy of vernalization.

Back in 1927, we had laughed hard at Fedorovich's description of Lysenko in *Pravda*. I burned the clipping a decade and a half later, though for warmth and not for spite nor even amusement.

It read:

If one is to judge a man by first impression, Lysenko gives one the feeling of a toothache. Stingy of words and insignificant of face, he has a dejected mien. All one remembers is his sullen look and his creeping along the earth as if, at the very least, he were ready to do someone in. Only once did this barefoot scientist let a smile pass, and that was at the mention of Poltava cherry dumplings with sugar and sour cream.

The great director had been noble, it is without doubt, but also willful. Courageous but also proud, high-minded but also deaf. There were so many warnings. An article appeared as early as 1931 on "applied botany, or Lenin's renovation of the earth." It denounced our institute as reactionary, unrelated to Lenin's thoughts or intents, inimical to them, alien in class. The great director's response was printed eventually, but only several months later and accompanied by editorial accusations that he concealed agricultural sabotage with the label of pure science.

Lysenko had already started to call the institute Babylon. "Babylon must crumble," he would say. "Dust."

The following summer, the government's decree on selection demanded that the required ten or a dozen years to develop cereals for different regions be reduced to four and that the crops be uniform and high-yielding. The great director spoke his skepticism, his voice cascading down to the heavy wooden table around which sat the men who mattered. Lysenko pressed his soft hand into his soft belly, stained his face with a smile, his swine eyes almost disappearing into skin. He promised to do it in fewer than three years.

Of course he could not, but doing mattered so much less than saying, something I tried to make the great director understand. He would only stare at me, pull his hand into a fist in such a way that it would twist the papers sitting on the surface of his desk, and whisper the word *mutant*. Mutated mutant, he would hiss.

And then he would say, so rationally, that science is not compromise. Things are either true, not true, or unknown. Yes, I would say, unknown.

But he always elected to ignore this and to continue by saying that he did not decide the results of his experiments before he conducted them. Once, he finished the conversation by saying, "There is nothing we can do but stand up for what is true, or at least state the truth and nothing else."

Of course, he was both right and wrong. He was right that we could not honestly say that we could produce what Stalin demanded in four years. But he might have found a way to say something other than no, hidden our disgust for Lysenko, who had seized on the class issue with all his surprising vigor – and with increasing success.

A few years later, Lysenko and the plagiarist Prezent announced a new concept of heredity to replace the old chromosome theory, which they denounced as reactionary, idealist, meta-physical, barren, and all things bad. Lysenko kept pushing his idiotic wheat vernalization and had farmers across the Union soaking their seeds and cursing their yields.

In 1939 the great director was denied papers to travel to a meeting in Scotland. He shrugged and declared he would rather spend the week collecting. At the Scottish meeting he did not attend, he was elected president of the International Congress of Genetics.

—

At least at first, I laughed when Lysenko called the institute Babylon. He meant to insult us as corrupt and decadent, of course, but I always heard it as a compliment. The ancient Babylonians had impressed me ever since I studied the early history of agricultural science back in the university.

Like the members of our own expeditions, the Babylonians traveled widely to collect medicinal herbs and unusual fruits. Either they or the Assyrians, who inhabited Babylon for a time, planted the world's first botanical garden. Babylonian agriculture was a thing of envy.

The ancient Babylonians ate dates, figs, pomegranates, apples, pears, and plums. They ate onions, leeks, garlic, and turnips, as well as cucumbers and lettuces. They made cheeses from the milk of sheep and goats and dined on game, pork, and mutton. Locusts were a delicacy. In old Babylon, no fewer than fifty kinds of fish were eaten, though fish apparently went out of fashion later, as the word *fisherman* came to mean something closer to *ruffian, opportunist.*

The Babylonians seasoned their food with mustard, coriander, and cumin. They had bread, oil, butter, beer, and eventually honey, and both red wine and white. Several kinds of grain, including a spelt, were also part of Babylonian meals.

But barley stood at the center of their diet

and was preferred over silver for exchange. When Hammurabi attempted to standardize interest rates, the rate for borrowed barley was much higher than that for a loan of silver.

Anything could be purchased with sacks of barley. It united wealth and weight, joined prosperity and health.

—

We were collecting spelt emmers in western Ukraine. A very old peasant, one of the few in the area who survived both collectivization and the hideous great famine to farm alongside his sons and daughters, directed us – based on the great director's description – to an untended field. We were searching for a plant we believed would reveal itself to be descended from one of the grains eaten by the Babylonians. The breeze wrapped cool around our shoulders, but the sun was warm on our heads and heat radiated near the ground. The day was, simply, perfect.

The Ford cars that appeared in the distance

and drew slowly larger shone like fat beetles against a field that was pressed low under the tall, late-summer sky. They crawled as close as they could. The men emerged in black suits and white shirts and dark ties, like the businessmen I had seen in larger American cities, except that their ties were thinner and not smoothly knotted.

Two of them flanked the great director, holding his arms in a way neither rough nor gentle but rather disinterested and insectlike. Two more took Sergei, which was surprising, for there were others among us who had spoken more sharply and more publicly.

They were back in the cars quickly, and the cars quickly gone, as though they had never come and our party had always been two men smaller.

I bagged the grain sample that the great director had dropped when seized. I remembered seeing Sergei's daughter at an institute picnic the spring before. A girl of four, maybe five years, she had stood with her back to me. I had registered only her hair, long and smooth and the exact color of the field from whence the spelt of Babylon had just been picked.

—

On July 9, 1941, the military collegium of the Supreme Court found the great director guilty of belonging to a rightist conspiracy, spying for England, sabotage of agriculture, and, proving that judges have a sense of humor, leadership of the Labor Peasant Party. He was sentenced to death. The meeting lasted several minutes.

—

The window of my New York apartment affords me a view of a row of Chinese markets. Instead of curtains, ducks – some uncooked and others glazed and roasted whole, with heads on – fill their windows. When there is no snow and no rain, the families who run the shops set out bins of foods that are mostly strange to me: dried cuttlefish and shrimp, fresh litchi nuts and foul-smelling but sublime-tasting durians.

People buy these things all day long.

—

A few blocks from my flat with Alena, in the direction of the institute, stood a posting board where people wanting to sell and buy could find one another. Before the siege, rectangles of paper, large and small, offered to sell all manner of thing, from bicycles to purebred cats to cookware. As the siege took hold and day followed day, the papers were most often tattered scraps. And food became the board's only subject.

By late November, no one found odd the little card offering a grand piano as payment for half a loaf of bread, though few were in the position to trade away anything that could be eaten for anything that could not – no matter how rare, fine, or beautiful.

There were other cards as well, offering more than musical instruments, referring out-right to bodies and souls.

I saw a woman, thin as everyone, spit in disgust upon reading such a notice. But its author plainly understood something the woman did not. The bravery to survive is a ruthless one. Martyrdom leads, by its very definition, only to the cold ground.

The only thing that struck me as truly strange about these postings was that they were not pulled down when the whole city ached for kindling. Neither was the poster of a woman holding a small, dead child that declared: DEATH TO THE KILLERS OF CHILDREN, though people risked the capital crime of picking up the flyers dropped by German planes, the flyers that outlined our surrender and prodded us to kill our leaders, give up, and eat again.

My own Alena brought home these flyers to start our small fires, telling me she would rather risk death and burn Hitlerite propaganda than set fire to even one page of her beloved books.

Of course the books would go too, one page at a time, from the title page of a less-favored novel and the dessert section of a cookbook after sugar could not be had to the dearest segments of the most precious classics – the plot turns of Turgenev, letters from the great director himself.

—

In the week before his death, Vitalii did not appear emaciated like so many, and it was not just because his face bloated. It was a though his body refused to burn its stores – holding on to them just a bit longer, just in case – and instead shrank around them, leaving pockets of fat like jokes in the midst of his gauntness.

Despite his tragic, comical appearance, he had been humorless for weeks. I am ashamed of my colleagues to say that there were some among us who held this against him, as though he owed not only his life but his cheerfulness to our all-important work.

But in his very last days, he only told jokes. He told Lidia the old one about the tombstone whose epitaph read: I TOLD YOU I WAS SICK. She burst into tears, and he laughed harder.

He told Alena highbrow jokes about philosophers and astronomy and me raunchy ones about strippers and widows.

He wouldn't stop joking and he wouldn't stop laughing, until, of course, he did.

The acting director arranged to have Vitalii's body taken away in a manner that he would have to repeat two dozen times, though some of our number did him the favor of dying at home. One young man, a research assistant in fruit breeding, was just never heard from again. We assumed that he had died anonymously. But I like to think that perhaps he merely slipped into another life somehow, or perhaps, like many, into insanity.

—

Rumors flew in unplanned and shifting patterns, like flocks of geese disturbed to the air by dogs.

We were winning the war; we were losing the war. We were losing the war because the German soldiers were stronger and better equipped; we were losing the war on purpose, part of our leaders' malevolent design. We were winning the war through heroism; we were winning the war with snow. Hitlerite soldiers would pour into the city in three days. On the streets of other cities, they were marching Russian heads on poles and taking their pick of the prettiest girls. They would bring food; they would take what food we had left. They felt special sympathy for Leningrad; they hated Leningrad above all and were saving special savageries for us.

And everywhere the hunger stories seeped, sewagelike, from office to office, home to home. Stories were told of tremendous sacrifice and honor. The man who gave up his own parcel of bread and oil to save an old woman's ration card from thieves. The mother who ate nothing for three weeks so that her children might take a bit more nourishment.

I took these stores with, so to speak, a grain of salt. I could see with my own eyes that deprivation debases more often than it ennobles.

I was more inclined to believe the stories of murder and cannibalism, however far-fetched they might have sounded only one year earlier. I believed the story of the man who killed his own brother for his ration card and then cooked him for meat. The story of the woman who self-amputated her leg for food. The story of the mother who starved her dullest child so that she might survive with her bright favorite.

I believed, in short, the stories about people who did things worse than I did, the stories about people less human (or perhaps more human) than I was.

—

Of all of us who endured after Vitalii's quick decline, Lidia was the one who changed the most and fastest. Lidia had been so beautiful that I would have married her instead of Alena had I met her first. As it was, I came very near – I fill with shame at how near – to leaving Alena for her.

But I was lucky that I did not, because the secret to Lidia's beauty was comfort. She was at her most beautiful, witty, and generous when her skin was warmed by the sun – and food was perched between her hand and mouth.

She was so subject to strong cravings that if she got a certain kind of cake in mind, she would walk clear across Leningrad to the bakery that made it best. She would leave work in the middle of the day to steam a fig pudding, coming back hours later with a riddle inside her broad smile. If it was me on her mind, she would have me in any vacant room or, barely concealed, outside.

My enchantment with her began during an

expedition to Malta, in the island's hottest month. I would allow my arm to fall on to Lidia's, gaze at the ribbon of her neck between her heavy, black hair and white clavicle, watch her dark lips while she tore *pan chocolat* with her strong teeth. She could eat three at a single sitting.

My Alena, with her more subtle, almost colorless attractions, had stayed home from that trip on account of the second of the babies that never came. After it was all over, I knew that I would stay with Alena until death divided us.

Yet on many nights, after Alena and I made love or if we did not, I would lie awake and think about Lidia's colors, her deep-bellied laugh, her vigorous appetite for sweets, her hips wide enough to pass infants.

But, as I have said, I am lucky, if you can call anyone who lived through Leningrad's starvation winter lucky – and, in truth, we all were – to have stayed with my small, dear, strong wife.

When Leningrad emptied of comfort and became only the case of a pillow on hard ground, all of its downy feathers blown away, Lidia's attractions, physical and metaphysical, gusted away as well.

Without comfort, her cleaver sarcasm was deboned into mere complaint. Without sun, her translucent skin turned sallow. Our trips to warm places had always kept her touched by air and sun, kept her skin clear, its white stained pink in just the right places. After the longest winter, she yellowed like inexpensive paper, and bumps rose from her forehead and chin. She had always carried a few more pounds than she needed. They had suited her, made her stomach soft and her bosom large, while the effort of collecting kept her strong.

Though she never got as skinny as some during the starvation winter – and I have my ideas about why this was so – she went slack with lack of food and exertion.

Of course, like so many, Lidia found ways to

eat. She had lost much of her charm, had lost the things that had come so close to tempting me away from my Alena, but still she was a woman and never an ugly one. For such a woman there was the possibility of associating with particular men, the kind of men who could still receive packages from Moscow with cans of evaporated milk, dried salmon, a square of chocolate.

And there was meat on the black market. Horse meat, it was said, but there could not have been more than one or two bony horses left in the whole city by the end of the hunger winter.

———

The bakeries produced a bread made of five parts' defective rye flour and one part each of salt, cake, cellulose, soy flour, hack dust, and bran. By November, the official ration for this vile loaf fell to 250 grams per day for manual workers, half of that for clericals and children.

No tree in the city had bark below the reach of the tallest man. It had all been stripped off and boiled for whatever nutrients it might contain and used as a salve for stomach pain.

All manner of animals – dogs and cats, sparrows and crows, rats and mice – and then their excrement were eaten. Soups were made from tulip bulbs stolen from the soil of the Botanical Gardens, pine needles, nettles, rotten cabbage, lichen-covered stones, cattle-horn buttons torn from once-fine coats. Children were fed hair oil, petroleum jelly, glue. Root flour and floor sweepings were baked into scones. Dextrin appeared in fritters, cellulose in puddings. Pigskin machine belts and fish glue were spirited from closed factories and boiled into jellies.

People did anything to feed their children. They traded away the valuable and sentimental. They killed and cooked beloved pets. They peddled their flesh. They peddled the flesh of the children needing to be fed. They stole, connived, and killed. They starved their spouses. They starved themselves.

So many times, dozens of times, I was told how lucky I was to have no children, how it was easier for us with fewer mouths to feed, not having to hear the horrible cries, to watch those we cherished more than anything, those who depended on us solely, suffer. Oh, the responsibility, people would say. And I would think, oh, the clarity.

I longed for the lucidity of parenthood during the bad time – maybe every measure as fully as Alena had hungered for the love and sweet smell of a baby before times turned bad.

The murky moral territory in which I stepped would have been another landscape entirely with children. Who faults a father for stealing if it is to feed his little child? A father tells himself this: I do what I must so that my child lives through this time. Parents may do anything at all and say this: We have to make sure our children survive, and we must survive to care for them.

I did not have this luxury. It did not matter if I lived, not even to me. Only I could not stand the pain that stood between me and death. It was that gray hunger, and not death itself, that I feared, avoided at the cost of all honor. As the smartest politicians repeat and know, ideals are nothing to the man who sits at an empty table.

—

"Are you angry with me?" Lidia asked me during the time that my Alena was wasting.

I laughed and shook my head. "No, Lidia, merely disenchanted."

"Yes," she said. "That's best. It's best that way."

This answer startled me, and I wondered if I knew her.

Lidia, as she had been, came often to my mind. I thought of her as a woman who could accept pain but not mild discomfort. Tie me up, she would say, make it hurt. Always more, harder, rougher. Her chest flushed when I gripped her wrist. Her lips reddened with pleasure when I bit her thigh. Turn me over, she would say, turn me over.

And yet she dissolved, character dissipating, personality irrelevant, unable to string together two thoughts, follow an idea, or laugh at a good joke the moment her stomach growled. She was undone by one early morning or a modest day's work. Thus she came to mind and I would think that I was just like her and then that, no, I was a different sort of person altogether.

—

A few weeks after the great director had been arrested and I had bagged the grain descended from the ancient Babylonians, Alena was visiting Sergei's wife, Vanessa. They spoke about strategies to win the release of Sergei and the others.

So many of us had been taken. Karpechenko, head of the genetics lab, a man whose school of thought had solved the problem of infertility in distinct hybrids. Govorov, who had been in charge of the legumes. Levitsky the cytologist. Hovalev, the director of the pest department and a leading breeder of fruit. Flykaberger, known for his expertise in wheat.

All in jail, if not dead.

Others had been deported by the new director, supported by orders from the commissar to dismantle the institute's departments and laboratories, to perform "productive" work on collectives.

So Alena happened to be sitting with Vanessa when they came for her, when they pried her daughter's fingers open to free her skirt from the little girl's desperate grip.

Alena was instructed to locate a relative to file guardianship papers within six days or to prepare the girl for the orphanage.

And so it was that Albertine, the girl with the

shiny, grain-colored hair, came to spend several days in our flat.

Without first consulting me, Alena moved the girl through our doorway. "She has no one else right now," Alena stated.

"Perhaps Vanessa should have thought of that." I despised the words even as they left on my breath. No one could have known that such things would be happening, that so many would be taken for so little.

Alena, as though sensing that I was already liberating myself, declined this line of argument. Instead she shrugged and simply, flatly repeated herself. "She has no one else."

I smiled at Albertine. She nodded at me but did not smile. Why should she, I asked myself.

"You'll sleep here until Mama and Papa come home, no?" I moved some of our bedding on to the sofa and organized it as best I could.

Albertine held Alena's hand and watched.

"Yes, you'll be strong until they come home?"

"Will they?" she asked not me but Alena.

Alena pressed her own small hands around the girl's small cheeks. "They will if they can."

It was Alena, not stoic Albertine, who permitted herself quiet tears.

—

Sometimes, to feel less false, I would remind myself – as though it made a moral difference, as though I was less odious because she was a scientist and not a club dancer or a waitress – that Lidia was one of the world's foremost authorities on the taxonomy of new-world beans, an expert on their relationship to the nitrogen-fixing bacteria that cleave to their roots.

In the Americas, on expeditions I had joined and on other trips, Lidia had collected hundreds of legume specimens. Since I had known her, she had often worn a few dozen examples, dried and strung as a necklace. She could finger each one and, without looking down, say its name and tell when and where she found it.

Her fingers on a compact black-and-white speckled bean, she would say, *Tarahumara carpinteria*, Nayarit, summer 1937. Touching a large beige bean with black mottling at the hollow of her throat, she would say, Hopi black pinto, middle mesa, Arizona, August 1936. And she could go on like that, her fingers making their way around the full circumference of her pretty neck, her mouth circling the strange words: Tohono O'Odham tepary, Zuni Shalako from the Sonoran desert, Quiche fava, *Tarahumara chókame* from Batophiles Canyon, Chihuahua. Her favorite, hidden behind her hair, was a tan tepary bean with deep blue speckles – a rare Mayan folkrace.

Once, in our earliest days. I asked her if she collected men like her bean beads and, if so, could she remember when and where she had picked each one. She had only laughed and said, "Naturally, and you are my favorite." A joke that ended my line of inquiry.

———

It was after I arranged for Albertine to be deported to distant relatives in France – an amazing feat for which I received no credit – that Alena signed the letter.

I had advised her not to sign, advice echoed by almost everyone, including the imprisoned director's brother, himself an important scientist. He is beyond help, I told her. Sergei and Vanessa are beyond our touch now. Albertine is safe, I whispered.

But a few, including Alena herself, I must admit, believed that she should sign the letter because she had no children and the others left did. The cruelest joke.

In the end, all the signatures save Alena's were removed. (My pen, wisely, had never signed.) The letter's sharpest points were sanded, but not so much that it was not still extremely dangerous, a tightrope walk over water vipers. Others had been taken in for much less. It was probably not enough to warrant a sentence of death, though in the two years prior to the blockade, that took very little if you were associated with the institute. And imprisonment could easily be death. Who would send food and blankets to a prison filled with garden-variety class enemies?

None of our number had been released yet. At the least, I thought, Alena would be put to labor on a collective.

I tried again, quietly, to dissuade her. He cannot be saved, I told her, not by you. You flatter yourself to think so. Those who have tried have succeeded only in joining him, I reminded her, and for all we know made his treatment worse.

Alena, even more quietly, completely without words in fact, resisted my wishes. And in the end, my fear of having her think me a coward overcame my other fears. I did not insist, for which I should be given some due. The letter was delivered.

She was taken from our apartment many weeks later, on a Sunday afternoon as we prepared a meal together. Her fingers were bright pink with the juice of a beetroot when she held her hand in farewell, my quiet wife again wordless and ever so brave.

I finished the cooking alone, basting the meat as it baked with sugar dissolved in vinegar, pounding the grated horseradish into a paste, slicing the beets my wife had boiled and peeled so that they stained my fingers the exact color of hers. I cooked the beet greens in fat until they fell apart. I cooled the food and wrapped it, though I could not be certain that I would ever see Alena again.

But on Tuesday, she returned on foot, exhausted and filthy but seemingly unharmed, her fingers still pink under the dirt. I warmed the food and set the table while she washed and put on a clean skirt and shirt.

Then we sat down to our belated Sunday dinner. The meat was sour from its extended contact with the cider vinegar, and I had overcooked the greens like I always did. But the meal was good nonetheless, and I was not alone.

The following day, Alena's salary was removed, and she was dismissed from the institute. She was lucky, everyone said.

In the coming year, Hitlerite Germany would put its iron kerchief around Leningrad's neck, and the definition of luck would fall even lower.

—

The first time I cheated on my Alena, it was brief, nameless, and far away from home. It was out of time, underground, undiscoverable, unrecognizable. It did not count, or it would not have counted except that I remembered it not only in my mind but with my fingers and nostrils and ears. I could not forget the texture of the skin, the up-close smell, the quality of voice – none of these better than my Alena's, but so certainly different.

I could never again tell myself that I had always been faithful, could never again take my wife's lovely hands, look into her eyes, and say, "I have been true to you, my wife."

And so, of course, others came, some at a great expense of conscience, some quite easily.

—

Cold in the skin. Cold in the bones of the arm. Cold in the eyes. Cold in the ribs. Feet gone from feeling, from knowledge. There was pain only in odd places, centered in a heavy, aching groin but otherwise intense in its asymmetricality, the finger of one hand, two knuckles on the other, a nostril's interior, a shrapnel-sized piece of jawbone, a small concentration in the kidney.

—

The hanging gardens of Babylon are believed to have been a magnificent and enormous quadrangle of lush foliage and flora, suspended atop stone columns, with trees rooted above the heads of men.

An homage of fecundity and water in an arid land, they were built in staggered terraces, arched vaults, and stairways. Their invisible irrigation system – an elaborate feat of human engineering hidden behind or under stone – revealed itself only in beautiful streams, water cascades and falls, permanently green grass, and the perfect smell of damp soil.

Sometimes we joked that our institute was the hanged garden of Leningrad. Unlike the famed gardens of Babylon, ours was not planted. We were mere and wonderful potential.

—

Eleven thousand starved in November. More than fifty thousand died in December, when wood for coffins was long gone. Daily I heard the dynamite crack, loosening the terrible frozen earth to sneak in the sheet-wrapped corpses, tall and short but almost all bone thin, pulled in on sleds, abandoned at the cemeteries for group burial. Too many to name or count or care about. But I would not come to such an anonymous end, I told myself, even then as though looking back from a great distance of years.

—

In a small town near the Pacific Coast, Alena and I had walked the square, taken in a colonial church with an unusually fine and simple wooden altar, and purchased a fabulous melon from a stall on the street.

The melon was unlike any I had previously encountered, and I have seen only one since, on another trip to Central America. It was large and oblong like a watermelon but with a pale, ridged, almost-white rind that made it look more like a winter squash than a summer fruit.

It grew heavy in my arms as we waited for the boat that would ferry us across half of Lake Nicaragua, to the island of Ometepe. There, a small band of us planned to collect what we could of the coffee, sesame, and strange fruits that grew in its fertile volcanic soil. We would also take notes on an unusual breed of cattle for some colleagues in Tbilisi and photograph some pre-Columbian petroglyphs by request of the culture ministry. Alena and I hoped to photograph some howler monkeys.

Heat was coming in with the day, and a pack of dirty boys pestered us for coins. The great director stood at the launch, looking out toward the two volcanoes that rose from the lake to form the largest freshwater island in the world. It struck me that he was seeking to put maximum physical distance – indeed all forms of distance – between himself and the little beggars.

I watched a woman just down the shore, washing the clothes on the rock. Unlike cheap travel paintings of boisterous women working and gossiping and splashing together, she was straight-faced and alone. She washed her family's clothes not as a social event but because they needed to be cleaned.

Sergei, loaded with bananas, distributed them to the beggars, and with the eating they again became boys, joking and playing hopping games with Sergei until the boat pulled close.

On the boat's deck, moving slowly toward the clouds and volcanoes of Ometepe, we cut into the melon.

I was surprised at Alena's appetite, which, four months into her first pregnancy, had been weak for some time. And the large lake's water was chopped by the strong, warm wind, making the boat jerk up and down. Yet Alena devoured slice after slice of the melon's rich orange flesh. Over and over, she said, "I've never eaten anything so good" and "Absolute ambrosia." And I thought: I do not know this woman at all.

I had such high hopes for us at that moment. I had already lied to her, of course, but I thought that along with the baby we would be delivered a new beginning.

Alena spit a melon seed into the sublime lake, warmth bathed us, and we were deeply happy for the last time.

What I realized only later, after seeing it again more than once, was that the return of Alena's appetite was caused by the plummeting of her hormones. She was no longer sick from pregnancy.

Alena miscarried the baby in a not entirely uncomfortable inn, in the middle of medical nowhere. She rested on the clean sheets that the innkeeper had insisted we accept while we waited for a boat to return us to real land. I sat at a table outside and watched our friends swim foolishly among the small but still dangerous freshwater sharks. I drank a sweet, purple drink made from pitaya fruit, and then beer after beer, and ate, grilled, three of the small fish that live nowhere in the world but Lake Nicaragua.

A local man used only a small stick to move a herd of a dozen or so cattle down the beach. I imagined him returning to a simple meal, a thick-waisted wife, and a vague number of small children. I would have traded places with him, at least at that moment. But of course he would not have agreed.

The great director sat with me, our bare feet in the sand that felt like dirt but fell away clean. "This island was once used for sacred burials. We are lucky that we do not have to bury Alena here."

He sat with me on the boat as I held Alena, and together we watched the volcanoes recede. I had planned to hike up into the cloud forest of the dormant Madera to see the lagoon in its crater. But now I focused on the perfect cone of the taller, still-active volcano, Concepción, and tried hard to feel worse for Alena than for myself.

The director personally arranged for the several forms of transportation we required, and Alena lived enough to arrive, unconscious and two days later, at the hospital in Managua. During some of the hours of waiting, I tried to picture what our lives would be and failed.

On the way home, there were other hospital layovers, in Atlanta and London. Alena would never again agree to travel pregnant, but, of course, the damage was already done.

—

Late, late, and I was alone, walking the corridor outside of the grain collections, my turn to guard.

I placed my feet slowly, heel rolling to toe, heel rolling to toe, making no sound myself, only remembering the sound of the great director's gait. Click, click, an even rhythm covering an uneven stride, longer on the right but faster on that side too, creating a symmetrical sound but a biased walk that had to be corrected by a step to the right about halfway down the corridor, where I now stood, shifting left so I could step right, imitating.

What I had thought of doing many times over the past weeks, I did now without thinking much about it.

Just a few kernels of a few kinds, taking nothing too rare, taking the last of no variety, rearranging the remainder to hide my weakness. My sore teeth, barely able to split raw rice, faired better with the soft pop of millet, the clean chew of teff.

Perhaps I had no right to the rice, no claim on the millet, but the teff was my find, mine to take back. I had collected it with my own hands on one of the first of my many trips with the great director. "Abyssinia," I said aloud, my mouth full. "Abyssinia."

Our steamer harbored in Djibouti the last week of 1926. The great director spent his night alone. Mine, I spent with a wide-eyed, French-speaking Somali girl with a smooth back and beautiful ankles. The next day we proceeded overland, by train, to Addis Ababa.

We were received by Emperor Menelik, who, it turned out, shared an interest in agriculture, wheat in particular.

He granted permission for our expedition as we ate our way through a procession of dishes, increasingly hot with spice: orange squash in coconut milk, mashed eggplant, raw marinated beef, lentils, mixed simmered greens, chicken-and-egg stew. We scooped mouthfuls of each with the thin stratum of fermented bread on which it was served. This *injera* grew like a sponge in my stomach, filling me far beyond comfort and pushing the meats and vegetables into my intestines too soon.

The flesh of my mouth – the insides of my cheeks, the softness under my tongue, and my palate more than my tongue itself – burned, pasted with powdered red pepper. My breath stung my eyes. I interrupted the great director, the emperor, his entourage, to retire.

The next morning, the great director woke me early to accompany him to the market to procure sandals for the fourteen men who would guide and serve us on our journey.

This was our second time on the errand, as the men, preferring money to shoes, had sold the first pairs given to them. An assistant to the emperor had advised us to leave the barefoot, shackled at the ankles so they would not abandon us in trouble, but the great director refused this course. I assured him that I understood his desire to give our men sandals instead of chains, but I urged him to consider local custom.

Always obstinate, always right, still malarial from recent travels in Syria and Palestine, he said he most certainly would not.

The air was still faintly cool, and few people were walking in the rows of the market when we first arrived. But more gathered with the growing heat, and it was difficult to push through with fourteen pairs of sandals, shoes for which I was sure we had parted with too much money. But we still had carte blanche in those days, and the director was not one to descend to argue with a stall keeper.

A week later, in the unmapped Ethiopian interior, when both of us were sickened with typhus on top of the malaria, our kindness was repaid. Our guides, shod, not shackled, did not leave us behind.

The director made one of his most pleasing finds on the road to Aksum, something previously unknown even through crossing: a stemless hard wheat that fit the law of homologous series. And I found the humble teff I now chewed dry in a cold Leningrad hallway.

The guides pressed us to return to the capital when our sickness worsened. As we were borne out of the interior, tied atop the mules that our guides considered unmanly to ride, the great director confided in me what he had been writing in his even script on page after page of his notebook. Ethiopia, he said, was indeed a center of plant diversity, and he was now certain that agriculture had been adopted from Ethiopia by Egypt and not, as most geneticists thought, the reverse.

He would be proved right, but he would be dead by then.

—

In the first days of the blockade, when people's notions of what mattered so altered, Alena asked the new director if she might come back, unofficially, just to do a little research. Nothing important, she stressed, and for no salary, just a little research on some landraces of rice. Genetics was her life.

The new director was not as devoted to Lysenko as we had expected. He was astute both scientifically and politically, which in these times meant he had only the narrowest line on which to walk.

Some of those who came with him, though,

held stupid ideas. Thick-nosed Ivanovich, who believed that all fertilization is useless because only soil texture influences yield, for example, was for a time given charge of vegetable breeding. His wife, Klavdiya, an angular, long-nosed woman who was much smarter than her husband, agreed with his every pronouncement, but always with a slight smile that hinted at irony, distance, disdain. I decided that I could perhaps cultivate her as a friend.

—

With the start of the war, we lost more in number than we added. All the young men went to the front, leaving only female students and then, later, the young men who returned injured.

Others were evacuated. I was surprised that the new director, who, it goes without saying, was very well connected, did not get himself evacuated. But not one of us could have known how bad it would get or how long it would last.

By the time we knew, it was far too late for most.

Of course the great director was gone too, long gone. Some said in Siberia. Others heard that he was actually in Moscow or had been evacuated to the more interior Saratov prison. His wife, Yelena, who was evacuated from Leningrad with their son, had not been told where he was.

The night before she left, she came to our flat to thank Alena for the letter she had signed. She did not thank me, though she must have known that I could have stopped Alena from signing had I really tried.

She told us that she did not expect to see her husband again. "One of us will be killed by the war or the prison," she said. "Possibly both by both."

I tried to soothe her, to give her the best to think, but my smart Alena shook her pale head. "No," Alena said. "She is almost certainly right. She will never see him again.

"We will keep up his work," Alena added,

and Yelena smiled, nodded, and pressed Alena's pretty hands.

Before his own arrest, the great director tried to help those who went before him. He put aside his own work, which for him was like putting aside his neck or his spleen, and wrote letters on their behalf. He made trips to Moscow and waited for hours to argue with men who did not want to listen to him or wanted only to hear him beg, which, of course, would never happen. He did everything else humanly possible, but there I must admit that some of it was out of stubbornness. He did not stop to consider that what he was doing might make things harder rather than better for those he wanted to help. But that is how idealists are.

In part because there was so much empty space from so many gone, Alena was allowed a corner of a basement laboratory and mostly ignored. When the watches of the collection were organized, she was given the harshest hours, at least at first.

After weeks passed, the political and even

scientific differences among us broke down. Weight and health became the important measures.

—

Before Lidia, the woman most dangerous to my marriage was Iskra.

Her mother had renamed her, as a girl, after the early Bolshevik paper. As a young woman, the name fit her well. She was indeed a spark. And I was combustible.

I traveled to Moscow whenever I could, indulging with Iskra in those things my pure, gently ascetic Alena would never touch.

We played tennis and dined on *pelmeni* and good wine and meat and cherry pies at the Prague Hotel while gypsy dancers performed under moving colored lights.

We smoked cigarettes and tapped our feet to Antonin Ziegler's Czech group at the Metropole, to Leonid Utesov and Aleksandr Tsfasman at the National.

Afterward, at Iskra's flat, I would carefully unhook – and roll down her beautiful long legs – the real silk stockings I brought back to her from my trips to France. I never knew what would come next.

At the parachute tower, on the day I fell in love with Alena, my future bride had told me that people use danger either to find themselves or to lose themselves. Perhaps the same is true of sex. With Alena, who needed neither to find nor to lose herself, sex was only sex, or perhaps potential procreation. She was wonderful to be with, always, and happy enough to make love. Despite taking her pleasure sadly, she enjoyed it for what it was. But not for anything more.

With no doubt, Iskra used sex to explore and express herself. She was different every time, and I thought that I might never tire of her and that it would be a good and safe thing to have only one mistress, whom I could eventually give up in older age for my wife.

But I did not give Iskra up for Alena.

I gave her up for Lidia, who, like me, sought in danger and sex not more but less of herself. In the weird mix of pleasure and pain that she always preferred, she abandoned the self that she must have hated as much as I, at least for a time, would come to hate it. As much as she wanted me to hate it.

—

For three days and part of the next, Alena did not speak to me except for the small phrases and questions necessary between two people inhabiting the same small place under hardship with no opportunity for one or the other to go elsewhere.

My offense was to have suggested, now that we lived under siege, that I had done Albertine a service by turning her out – though *turning her out* was Alena's phrase and not my own. Now Albertine dined on roast duck and *rampions* and good bread while the children of Leningrad lived as orphans in the

Caucasus or chewed sawdust or their own tongues.

Alena, of course, was right that I could not have known that the blockade was coming. But I had always been right that France was a better place for a little girl whose parents had been jailed as internal enemies. And I could not understand why Alena seemed angrier with me now than she had when Albertine first departed.

On the fourth day of this treatment, I placed my hands around Alena's vanishing waist and kissed the side and back of her nape. My wife had never turned away my affections, and even now, when she hated me, she accepted my hands, my mouth, and the rest of me, sharing what remained of her body with me.

Of all the things I have to be ashamed of, this one comes to mind as often as any other.

—

Contrary to the imaginative indulgences of Herodotus, the Babylonians prized sexual fealty.

Infidelities were punished harshly, but there was room for forgiveness. Though an adulterous wife caught in the act was usually bound to her lover and drowned in the Euphrates, her husband could grant her pardon. I have wondered how often that happened – and how often for love, how often for revenge.

If a wife went off with another man after her husband was taken prisoner, she was to be drowned, unless she did it for hunger. If she went with the other man because there was no food in her house – if she was lured by his pantry and not his bed – then no blame whatsoever was attributed to her. It has always been understood that people need to eat.

—

The herbarium was now mostly dark below its single row of high windows. The air by the ceiling, though, held dirty afternoon light. I was alone, but the cracking sound brought me unease, brought fear of exposure.

Even though the rice was raw and stung my tender gums, its nutty flavor filled me with warmth and pleasure inside my skin of cold and discomfort.

This variety of rice grows in the humidity of southern Louisiana, and it was there that we – the great director, Lidia, Sergei, a whole little expedition of us – collected it in addition to several wild landraces. The trip was my last good time with Lidia.

Rice was Alena's specialization, but she had stayed in the pure air of Leningrad, waiting there to study the fruits of our collecting. In Louisiana, where the air is of another quality altogether – outside of time and living and breathing with heat and moisture – there is no pure, no impure. Most of our skin lay visible to the touch, and nothing seemed wrong. . . .

I stopped, having eaten more than I set out to, having wakened rather than dulled my painful appetite. I longed to take home the small mound of pecan rice left in my palm, to boil it in water, to salt and sugar it and feed it in steaming spoonfuls to my Alena.

But I knew that she would close her lips to the food.

—

On my way from the institute to our flat, I watched a mother walk hand in hand with her newly mature daughter. Their proximity seemed to please them both, and yet I felt the mother's hand commanded the daughter closer than she would like to be.

They turned and disappeared from my view behind the rump of one of the stone lions that presides without interest over the Catherine Canal.

—

In 1776, south of Baghdad, peasants found the unfinished basalt figure of a lion amid the ruins of what was once Babylon's northern palace. This lion stands hard, trampling the hapless

man who lies beneath his paws. Unlike the
seated lions that gaze so elegantly at the
Catherine Canal, the Babylonian statue was
made by someone whose gods were intimately,
if cruelly, involved with human fate and the lots
of individual men.

—

Alena stood across the room from me, and I
saw her in relief. She spit softly on to a cloth
and wiped, slowly, one by one, the cacti from
the Botanical Gardens that she had agreed to
care for. She kept them as warm as she could
with our paltry fire and kept their pores open
by rubbing them with her own saliva each
day.

I watched and swallowed my own spit to
diminish the hunger nausea that I could never
move past.

Though Alena's hair was thinned and oddly
parted from multiple nutrient deficiencies,
from the room's distance I could see only that

it was as long as it had always been. And backlit by the window, it appeared luminous.

But the window told everything. At the start of the terrible winter, we had tacked layers of butcher paper over it to keep some of the cold outside, only to punch holes and tear the paper into kindling to keep our books from the fire.

So the light that revealed Alena's former prettiness came through ripped and broken like the paper.

—

The finest piece of fruit I have ever eaten was in Colima, in western Mexico. Twin volcanoes smoking in the distance, the perfect whitewash of a colonial square in the foreground.

It was a mango, bought off the street, skewered on a stick barely strong enough to support its weight. The old man who sold it to me slashed it quickly, artfully, with a knife that seemed much too long for the job. He achieved brief, crisscrossing incisions just shallow of the hardened flesh around the seed. His precise cuts formed perfectly biteable pieces, only a shade too large – and marvelously so – for the mouth.

"Just bite off a little more than you can chew," I said to the great director.

But when he looked at me, his eyes did not register the joke. The old fruit vendor smiled, though I am sure he understood not one word of Russian. But he was a man who understood tone, inflection, subtlety, intent – the real meaning of a situation, all that happens between two people.

He sprayed the mangoes with salt and chili powder and lime juice to make us realize the perfect sweet flavor of the fruit itself.

And we did. Even the director moaned slightly, happily, deep in his voice box, his eyes narrowing and almost shining.

The mangoes in upper India were something altogether different. Smaller, greener, more fibrous. Better for putting up than eating fresh, often too sour. But the one I ate after a long night of fighting, touching, fighting, touching, fighting Lidia was too sweet.

Again bought from the street, this one came from the hands of an old woman. Hands not so different from the hands of the elderly Mexican man who had shaken chili powder on the best piece of fruit I have ever eaten.

But her hands moved differently. Precise also, but unconcerned. Just a piece of fruit to be eaten by just a man.

And she served it differently. The mango was already halved and pitted. She cupped it in her hand and scored the flesh into dice, almost to the skin. She lifted her fist as though to strike a hard blow to my face. When I only stood there, staring, she grabbed by hand, formed it into a fist, and punched it for me into the skin of the mango half. The diced pieces spread from my fist like armor. Bite, bite, she said, pretending from a distance to bite off a cube, her small blackened teeth snapping the air.

It was a clever way to open a mango, and the

pieces were entirely manageable. But the taste spread unpleasantly in my mouth. Somehow both sour and much too sweet.

I spat out the yellow pulp, and the woman looked at me with supreme satisfaction.

It was her gaze and the taste in my mouth and that yellow color spat out on the street that brought back the sickness from Abyssinia. The malarial mango, I would always think of it.

So it was the other mango, the Mexican one, that I tried to conjure as I scraped with my small penknife at the hard dried core of a mango whose fruit was long gone. My efforts produced little, but I had better luck forcing the seed across the broken surface of a little device designed to grate nutmegs that I had picked up while traveling in Iberia.

Only when I had fully obscured the bottom of a small bowl with powdered mango pit did I stop. I added warmed water, hoping to soften the shavings and make a paste. But the water and the seed remained distinct, refused to blend. So I settled for drinking the dirty water.

Like always, my regret was instant. I do not mean the guilt of theft and survival, which was constant, but simple regret for having awakened the horrible hunger that had finally gone numb.

I told myself that pain was the price of life; its absence was the step into death.

—

There are many ways to manipulate seed dormancy and germination, to shorten or lengthen the vegetative periods of cereals. Seeds can be stratified, brought out of dormancy with an imposed change of temperature. Scarification – the nicking and scratching of the hard seed coatings of plants such as morning glory and okra – can end dormancy and begin germination so long as care is taken not to damage the embryo within the coating.

And even Lysenko's infernal vernalization

has its uses. Soaking wheat in certain conditions until it is swollen can shorten, by a few days, the vegetative phase of some spring varieties, thereby slightly increasing yields if the second half of summer is dry. But it is time consuming and wastes seed. It causes some varieties to fail outright, and should summer's second half be moderately wet, yields will fall.

By the time the war started, Lysenko himself had quietly dropped vernalization, but not before he had made it an issue of class and turned Stalin against all of genetics. What the cost of this would be, I could only guess. But the ends of wars bring change, and this was what we had to rest our small hope upon.

—

"Stop by my office when you have a few minutes," he had said. And so I found myself knocking on the door of the new director, a man who had no doubt earned his position through both ability and libel, hard work and treacherous cunning, good luck and petty remarks.

Sitting in a surprisingly comfortable chair, I watched the man and the driving snow through the window behind him. The man was my age and just barely remarkable. He would have been unremarkable, but he was just a bit slighter of frame and more handsome than what might be considered average.

"The delightful wife of Ivanovich speaks highly of you. She feels you to be a most useful colleague."

Be careful, I told myself. In those times, one day's patron was the next day's doom. "It pleases me to hear these words, certainly, though I am not particularly well acquainted with Ivanovich's wife."

"But what I really wanted to tell you, why I asked you to stop in, is what Pryanishnikov has been up to since he managed to get himself evacuated from Leningrad."

"Ah, that's right, I had forgotten that he had

been evacuated." I said this in a way so as to seem disinterested, or better, interested only in passing and upon being reminded.

"And of course you know that our disgraced former director was a student of his back in the old days."

"I knew that, yes, at least at one time. But I have not thought of such connections in many years." I met the new director's gaze, but tried not to hold it beyond a moment, letting my eyes refocus on the ever-stronger snow.

"It seems that Pryanishnikov has gone and nominated his star pupil for a Stalin prize."

Against every voluntary physical power, I laughed loud and hard.

"You find that funny."

I could not stop laughing. Finally, I managed to say, "Funny is exactly what I find it. Would you not say that it is funny that a man in prison is nominated for a Stalin prize?" My boldness so surprised me that I thought it possible that I had been insane for some time and was only now noticing it.

The director began to laugh with me – a shrill, ringing laugh like a mynah bird. Despite its peculiar tone, it seemed genuine enough. But the director stopped so abruptly that I realized it must have been false. "It is indeed funny," he said.

He stared at me for a time. His eyes were pale blue, but speckled with dark spots of green and black. His gaze was softer than I might have expected, almost kindly. Then he looked down and began to read through some stapled papers on his desk.

I watched the snow, still hard, small, and driving in at an angle. "Was there something else you wished to speak to me about?" I asked.

He looked up, as though startled to see me still sitting across from him. "I merely wanted to know what you thought about the disgraced former director, whom I know you worked closely with, being nominated for a Stalin prize.

And now I know: you think it is funny." He returned to his papers.

As I was leaving, he looked up one more time and said, "Oh, and how is your fine wife?"

"Well enough, thank you," I said. "We are getting by as well as anyone – no worse, no better."

—

Among the evacuees of 1942 were the great director's wife and son, who were settled in Saratov. They were told that the great director was imprisoned in Moscow, when he actually slept, malnourished, only a few kilometers from them. Did they feel his proximity or are such things not possible, I wondered later, when I heard.

His death sentence commuted but his death imminent, he was moved from Saratov prison to Magadan, where his cell was chilled by the cold but unseen Sea of Okhotsk. The precise details would never emerge, but he certainly died of mistreatment and malnourishment, perhaps more of one than the other, in late January of 1943.

When he arrived in my dreams or in my waking mind as if in dreams, he appeared emaciated, pocked by the hunger edemas of lengthy albumin starvation. He appeared as my Alena had one year earlier.

—

My Alena survived the winter of hunger. In early March, I stood in Sennaya Square. It had been underwater in 1924, when people had waded neck deep, carts floated, and horses were forced to swim.

The square had been under food in 1934, when the new economic policy claimed credit for the bumper crops of cabbage, greens, and root vegetables. Carriage wheels and horseshoes locomoted dry over the flagstones of Nevsky-Voznesensky Prospect.

Submerging the square now were coffins –

less scarce despite the wood that was still scavenged for warmth and the bodies that still succumbed to months of wasting, even after being fed bread and broth and potatoes. Even after more than one million left the city, evacuated against the currents of oil and electrical charge that now surged into Leningrad through pipeline and cable across Lake Ladoga, our road of life. Even now, after food was almost not scarce and newspapers prepared to print and small signs pronounced the imminent reopening of theater, cinema, and production house.

Still skin tore open to edemas and bowels drained faster than mouths could drink.

Alena had never had many pounds to spare. My dear, small Alena, whose only extra flesh curved in a few crescents. The crescents that were the bottom halves of her breasts, the crescent low on her abdomen made by the babies that had not been born, the slivers where her legs met her body. These beautiful bows remained for a time, even as her flesh caved through her ribs and her arms shrunk into matchsticks, snappable.

Now that the city recovered and my Alena did not, now toward the end, I rested my hands, sometimes the side of my face, on these last purses of flesh to stop myself from climbing on top of her and using up the strength that she lost so fast, to stop myself from using up the last of her.

—

According to ancient records, stone, otherwise almost unheard of in ancient Mesopotamia, was twice used to build in Babylon. Stone was incorporated in the north wall of the city's northern citadel. And stone slabs – covered by layers of reed, asphalt, tile, and metal – were used in the foundation cellars of the hanging gardens. The mud brick that constructed most of the rainless city would have eroded away under the gardens' impressive irrigation and flowing channels.

There exists more than one theory about which ruler should be credited with the gardens, and when they were built and why. Some believe they were built by the Assyrian queen Semiramis centuries before Nebuchadrezzar. For some time it was thought that Senaherib was the mind behind them. And many historians, noting that the gardens are mentioned only by later Greeks and appear nowhere in the Babylonian record, have argued that they never existed.

But the most widely accepted version has it that they were conceived by Nebuchadrezzar as a gift to his homesick queen, Amyitis. Originally from Media's lush green mountains, Amyitis found the brown baked flatness of Babylon depressing and pined for home.

What can be sure about the hanging gardens is that – whoever ruled at the time, whichever brilliant mind conceived of their unexpected lushness – the stone slabs that form their base were laid by slaves, also homesick, pining for wives they either would or would not see again.

—

I remember Alena's last meal: a roll made from rye flour and a bowl of broth made by boiling garlic, carrot peelings, and one fat, perfect potato in salted water. She trembled when I set the hot bowl before her, steadied her hand by resting it on the roll, laughed in a laugh I had never before heard as she breathed in the soup's steam. "It will be funny if I wait," she said.

It was the most frightening thing I have ever heard.

"I will wait for half an hour," she said. She waited, but only for a few minutes, before drinking the bowl dry and eating the roll gone.

—

During the hunger winter, I was justified to take what I needed, and I barely took more. I had to discipline myself to remember this truth only a few months later, after my Alena and the others died, making way for those remaining, now all reasonably well fed.

Survival did strange things to people – I knew this. Viktor from the cytology laboratory, who had always been generous, always quick to give away even something he needed, to accept blame but not credit, suggested that we deserved our lives for some reason, obvious or occluded.

Lidia, who had always been generous only to herself and seemed well on her way to madness said that was not so, but that we must behave as though what Viktor said was true.

I held neither position, believing only in meaningless fortune most of the time, or acknowledging simply that I had been willing to do more to save my life than some of those who had died – a trait that made me neither better nor worse than any other man or woman.

—

I can admit that the deprivation was even harder for Lidia than for me. For me, the pain was fear of slow death. For Lidia, I believe it was sheer physical and emotional torment.

At first she just went sour, but then came meanness, followed by the madness. I thought she would warm with the weather when the first winter finally, finally broke, and sun melted the snow, and there was a little more food – some grown in Leningrad, some lorried across Lake Ladoga in the last weeks it was frozen. Bread came out of the Kirov bakery. Rations were strict, but enough to keep those still healthy alive.

But Lidia did not return to herself. She got more and more desperate even as things improved. The extra food she had managed to get – and I continued to have my suspicions about how – had kept her weight on, even added a few pounds back, but did not stop the scurvy sores from appearing on her arms.

By the second winter, when my Alena was many months gone and I might have yielded to Lidia's comfort, she was not lucid. She rarely left the institute, and she would not take off her once glorious but now filthy sable coat. Like all of us, she carried a rod to beat off the rats, but unlike the rest of us, she looked equally willing to strike human beings.

And of course she had refused to speak to me since she discovered me with grain in my mouth.

—

Lidia was not the only one to have found me out during the hunger winter.

One evening, as I began my watch, the wife of Ivanovich was concluding hers. "Perhaps I should stay and guard you," Klavdiya said, smiling, solicitous.

My heart seemed to beat sideways. Brief images of a dozen places I had been in my life tumbled through my mind: the second row of a streetcar in New Orleans as it passed a certain blue house, a particular crook in the port at Fez, a small store on the other side of Leningrad, a hallway in Moscow. Each vividly specific, felt in the body.

"I'm quite sure I don't take your meaning" is what I replied through the corporal memories, now all Leningrad. That charming spot by the River Moyka, the European height of Lomonosov Square, the spreading, clean, red-and-green angles of Pushkin Square.

"None of that. No pretense between scientists." She smiled and added, "But you have no need to deny anything. I will not tell anyone what you are doing, why you weigh more than your wife. I merely wanted you to know that I know. And understand."

I wanted to ask what she meant by *understand.* How did she know? Was she guessing, or could she tell because she was doing the same thing? A sneak spots a sneak.

"Not me," she said, "not the same. But I do understand. We all have our ways. Now I know yours and you do not know mine."

I paced for hours, too frightened to touch a

single grain of anything until the first hint of morning, when I was unable to stand the proximity of food any longer. I chewed a few, just a few, seeds of sunflower and melon.

—

More than twenty of us died, the majority during or at least from the winter of hunger, but a few later from Hitlerite shells.

I am not counting those who died or rotted slowly in prison – not counting the great director, not counting Sergei or Vanessa, not counting so many who, of course, count and should be accounted for on some other register.

But they are another list, a different group. They belong to the life before. The siege destroyed continuity as much as it destroyed all of the other ideas it ruined. There would always be before, during, and after. And nothing would ever bridge the three.

Among those who began the siege but did not come out the other side of that concrete space were friends and enemies, my beloved wife, and men and women I barely knew outside of their research results. Some were perfect to work with. I think now of Ilya, one of our bureaucrats, a man with a gentle nature and a wide and dry humor. He poked fun at everyone equally, and treated everyone with true respect. I think also of kind and earnest Natalia, who was beautiful into early old age.

Some of those who died were annoying, such as fastidious Anton, always more concerned with the inventory and cleaning of equipment – and with not being exposed as a second-rate mind – than with getting any real work done. Some, such as stern but brilliant Efrosinia, I had never given much thought to. But I would come to honor all of them as they shrank and grew ill before me.

And I miss each of them, even Anton, with his round-eyed defensiveness and ridiculous little beard. More than many of the things I might want, I would like to run into Anton in the street, buy him a drink, and talk about old times and new. Perhaps now, both smoothed by long years of living, we could be great friends.

But of course Anton turned out to be brave and strong, and so he died while he was still unlikable.

—

Only a few years ago, I ran into Leppik, the mycologist who had guarded some of our collections at the Estonian experimental station. We were both at the Botanical Gardens for a seminar on microtoxins. One of the presenters spoke of a case in the Middle East. Others talked about the possibility that unfriendly governments were using microtoxins to develop agents of biological warfare.

The talk that most interested me – and the one where I saw Leppik – was about the *Fusarium* poisoning that hit Byelorussia at the end of the war with Hitlerite Germany. A crop of millet had been left unharvested through the wet winter. By the time it could be collected in spring, it had molded, but there was little else left to eat. Perhaps a million people, perhaps not quite so many, died from the contaminated grain. Some died from direct poisoning, others from secondary infection. But most died from asphyxiation caused by the swelling of their throats.

Fusarium does not, it is believed, enter the milk of nursing mothers, so small babies were spared. But it does survive the brewing process, and a number of people were sickened or killed from drinking beer.

Leppik invited me for a coffee after the seminar. We avoided the past, though the mycologist did tell me about his efforts to make the great director's theories known to American scientists. We made no plans to meet again.

—

Everyone I overheard spoke of the concert. The score would be brought to Leningrad by plane, it was said. Because only sixteen of more than one hundred were left in our orchestra, the military was granting leave to professional musicians, even from the front. Practicing trumpeters blistered their lips with cold mouthpieces. Eliasberg would conduct but was deeply worried about the stamina of the surviving and arriving musicians. One flutist and a trombone player were so emaciated that they could not sit on their chairs without cushions. The symphony was quite strenuous, it was said – Shostakovich's finest work. "He's always been a true Leningrader," some said.

Of course many layers of human pettiness returned with food and warmer weather. As appetites shrank and the sun warmed bodies, I heard whispers that the symphony was not really so fine, that many in Moscow were not so impressed, that inferior musicians were seeking opportunities that should never have been open to them.

The date was set for the ninth of August.

Those stationed at the headquarters of the forty-second Soviet Army were ordered to prevent shelling that night no matter the cost. They would take out German artillery, it was said. Music would spare the city. It would save not only our souls but our bodies and buildings.

It was Klavdiya who offered me a seat. "My husband cannot attend, and I require an escort."

I nodded. I was not a music lover and could not be comfortable with a woman who knew what I had done, what I was. But neither could I resist vanity and history. The Philharmonic Hall was the place to be. The concert sold out rapidly.

Klavdiya sat to my left. A gas mask sat on the lap of the man to my right. A woman behind held one to her face. People wore their former finery, most often as rags. Men and some women carried guns.

The bombardment subsided. Eliasberg lifted

his baton, his oversize tux hanging off his arms comically, tragically. Instruments were placed on the stage's many empty seats, both a tribute to the dead and a suggestion of fuller sound. I stared at an orphaned piccolo as the first movement began its savage march.

At the end of the second movement, I felt Klavdiya's long fingers climb on to my arm. I let them remain, but only that.

The strings bounced, almost jaunty, then gave way to Ksenia Matus' sad oboe. A bassoon entered, and then the oboe disappeared under the returning strings, which tore open a pizzicato melody. They were joined by clarinets, one shy, and then brass, not quite strong enough but brave indeed, and the flutes.

No one spoke, and it seemed that no one breathed. The Hitlerite shells did not fall. At the end, applause, sobbing, Eliasberg's wild grin.

I might have succumbed to Klavdiya, but she chose the wrong time and place: that night of homage to Leningrad's weakness and strength, in the flat that I could think of only as Alena's, on the sofa that had been for so few nights little Albertine's bed.

I accepted Klavdiya's full-lipped kiss, her cool hand inside my shirt, her breath in my ear, the knowing tip of her hips into my leg. But when she paused to say that we should be together because we were so much alike, I pulled away.

"No," I said. "For that very same reason, we should never pair. If we are alike, we should stay far apart."

I had never refused an even mildly tempting offer of indulgence, so I was unsure what would follow. I expected anger but instead saw resignation. Perhaps even understanding. For the many years I would know Klavdiya, the night of the symphony would always be between us, as though everything had happened and nothing had happened. As though both versions were true at the same time.

—

During the summer of 1943, kittens were bought and sold through the posting board near my flat for as much as two thousand rubles. They were no longer eaten, but in demand to kill the rats, themselves once scarce protein, now a nuisance. No one in Leningrad would now eat a rat or admit to ever having done so.

The Botanical Gardens' famous palms were dead, but its lime trees bloomed in June. I finally returned the cacti that my Alena had saved with her own saliva and touch and that somehow survived first my inattention and then my attention. I was thanked profusely by her friends there. A brave woman, a remarkable scientist, a pure mind. Yes, I nodded, all of that.

By July we had strawberries, red currants, raspberries, veal, dill, baby turnips, marrow. Mussolini resigned, and Italy capitulated. Roses could be had.

August brought late lilacs and rains fine as

hair. But the shellings turned more deadly as the Germans, sensing a turn and knowing that the first shell is always the most dangerous, tried to kill more of us by exchanging long, almost boring shelling sessions for many short ones. I would hear the whistle, then the burst, then scan the white sky for the pillar of smoke, colored by whatever was hit. Sometimes the smoke would be the gray of stone, the red of brick. Sometimes it was the precise, unlikely hue of human flesh.

On my way to the institute, after a series of shellings occurred not so very far from our flat, I saw an arm, separated from an unseen woman, holding a still-burning cigarette. The availability of tobacco signaled better times to come, I thought, and then castigated my mind for the direction it had traveled.

A block further along, I saw a man on a stretcher, the left half of his head gone and stuffed with cotton wool, as though the fabric could sort numbers, direct his limbs, feel pain, remember a beloved.

—

Two millennia before Christian-measured time commenced, the Babylonians began to celebrate their New Year every spring. The eleven-day festival of gloom and purification and finally joy came to be known in later Babylonia as Akitu. It was believed that the gods ended each festival by setting human fortunes for the coming year.

I always liked the idea of the Festival, or Mardi Gras, celebrated in Catholic countries, with full debauchery preceding the purification of self-denial and with people in at least tenuous control of their own fate.

One of Leningrad's most important celebrations came not in spring but on the anniversary of the October revolution.

And of course our gods, if we had any – and no one could claim that we did – were not interested enough to set the lots of individuals. Ours was a collective fate, and we had suffered and survived.

This year's festival was less energetic, of course, yet also less dour than before we had suffered. People wore brighter colors: it seemed that everywhere I looked, I saw yellows and reds and purples. Women adorned their hair with fabric flowers, and people lacking access to more valuable ornaments pinned pieces of colored paper to their shirts. Relief was everywhere spoken and felt. Signs read: I AM HERE and WE HAVE SURVIVED.

I remembered one of the banners from the Gorky Park celebration: HE WHO DOES NOT LAUGH, DOES NOT EAT. Now the sign would have to read: HE WHO DOES NOT EAT, DOES NOT LAUGH. The joke, of course, would have been on all of us.

—

Within a generation of Hammurabi's rule, an Indo-European people known as the Hittites swelled with military and political power. In 1595 B.C., Hittite armies marched to Babylon from Anatolia and sacked the great city, bringing the old Babylonian empire to its humiliating end.

But the Hittite king, amid ugly internal politics, abandoned Babylon, returning to his own capital and his almost immediate assassination.

Thus Babylon was left to the Kassites, who ruled it for four centuries.

Babylon was sacked again in 1225 B.C., this time by the Assyrians, who kept the city for only seven years before its citizens successfully revolted. Again, Babylon had its indirect revenge: the Assyrian king was murdered by his own circle for bringing evil onto Babylon, whose city god was now worshiped by Assyrians as well as Babylonians.

But it would not be long before the Assyrians – notorious for their brutality and population redistributions – brought more suffering to Babylon. Their long and bloody struggles with the Egyptians led to a siege of the city that lasted almost precisely as long as the siege of Leningrad would, so many years later.

Within two decades, the Assyrian empire fell after only a three-month siege of its capital, Nineveh. Then, in 550 B.C., the Persian king Cyrus the Great sacked Babylon yet again, this time killing off the Babylonian empire once and for all.

—

By the midpoint of December, Leningrad still had not seen the winter's first blizzard. But it was cold as I stood outside, looking up through the very last fragment of daylight, at the window of our flat, imagining Alena just inside the paper, cleaning her small, important collection of cacti, caressing the succulents, never pricking her fingertips.

But I was not deluded. I knew that she was not there but gone forever. My eyes moved up the façade of the building to the open square of blackening sky above, and I saw the aurora borealis of the new winter for the first time.

The colored lights were not as spectacular as they sometimes are, as they are when I have to remind myself of their scientific explanation to stop from staggering.

No, this night they were soft and appeared hand tossed. Lofted by small strong fingers.

One afternoon when Albertine was with us, I entered the flat and found Alena sitting on the floor. Albertine sat on a chair behind her, brushing and braiding her shiny pale hair. They looked up at me briefly, but otherwise ignored me.

"What happens to my mother and father if they die?" Albertine asked, taking a thick plait of Alena's hair in her mouth.

"There are many answers to that. People believe many things."

Albertine firmly took the plait into her hand, spitting out a loose piece of hair, showing her first impatience. "That I know, but who is right?"

"It depends on where they live and who rules them," I said.

Albertine gave me the longest, clearest gaze she ever had and nodded.

"No," said Alena. "Only one answer is right. It's just that we don't know which. I believe you will see your parents again."

"If anywhere, not here," said Albertine.

—

When they spoke of it, and they spoke of it seldom, the Babylonians described the place of the dead as a place where dust is nourishment, clay is food. Convinced that their sins would be punished in this world, this life – whether by men or by gods – they had little use for hell.

—

People suffer, of course, but less for their sins than for merely being human. More often than not, we get away with our crimes. Our slights are forgiven by those we slight. Our secrets remain secret. We blaspheme, and lightning does not strike.

Exceptions, of course, abound. Sometimes in life, as in literature, people get their just deserts. The greedy man loses everything because he cannot resist seeking more riches. The town gossip is undone by her own tongue. The merciless judge must beg quarter for his personal sadisms.

But usually fate is not so direct, and there is no one to punish us if we do not punish ourselves.

I had enjoyed so much pleasure in my life. I tried to remember the names of the women whose pleasure I would trade for one last hour with my Alena, in health or even in sickness. Some I could remember and some I could not. And I knew that the trade I desired was not available to me.

Now that I avoided Lidia and had turned down Klavdiya, I could only laugh at my belated fidelity. The Americans I know like to say, "Better late than never," but this means nothing to me.

—

Klavdiya was turned more toward the window than from it, so I could see less than her profile against the day's gray light. It was a spy's view that revealed only one odd angle of an entire woman.

Yet with nothing more to go on, no slumped shoulders, no downward dip to her chin, I could see that she was both very sad and very tired. The sadness seemed deeper than the tiredness, below and behind it, the sadness the cause of the tiredness and not the other way around.

She did not startle when she sensed my presence, and she waited a few moments before turning.

"My husband was killed by a shell," she said. "Ivan is dead."

I cannot say what I felt, and my memory of it as only an emptiness makes me worry that I felt nothing at all. "I did not realize, until maybe now, that you loved him."

"Of course I loved him," she said, and

returned to her odd watch over the view outside her laboratory window, a view I knew so well but for the life of me cannot remember.

—

When the Leningrad front offensive was officially announced, all the lucky citizens of Leningrad could feel that the blockade would soon enough be broken, could feel like a pulse the trembling of the ground caused by the Soviet naval guns, continuous, nearly subliminal, and life preserving.

Every day the radio chanted and droned the names of the liberated communities. Krasnoy Selo, Ropsha, Peterhof, and Duerhof; then Uritsk, Ligovo, Strelna, and Novgorod. All places where people lived, I thought.

We heard reports of the sappers who, with their trained dogs, searched for mines in the liberated outlying areas of Leningrad, all now treeless, covered with only the lowliest vegetation.

Soap was being made again, and the piano

factory would soon be running. Also, every day, both morning and afternoon, came the radio committee's advertising for trumpeters and piccolo players. The dead still had not been replaced. Forgotten perhaps in a necessary amnesia, but not replaced.

Pushkin and Pavlovsk were liberated on the twenty-fourth of January, and then, three days later, Leningrad, emancipated, rejoined the living world.

That night more than three hundred guns fired twenty-four salvos. At first only green rockets were used, and the sky glowed, phosphorescent like the Gulf of Mexico with its tiny ethereal dinoflagellates and ctenophores. Then it flashed red, and next gold like jewelry, shining and reflecting white as the searchlights of ships lightened the whole weight of the sky.

—

Lidia declined a post in Moscow, instead lobbying for and landing a quiet research position in Tbilisi. I learned of the success of her plan only upon seeing her packing boxes. The muscle on the front of her arm twitched below her dark sweater as she hoisted a full box from the floor to her desk. Her black hair had been shorn at an angle just below her chin, which made it look as thick as it ever was. Under it, her skin had cleared, though it was still unstained with color, even with the physical effort of lifting the heavy box.

Behind her were the microscopes and petri dishes full of agar that she would leave for microscopes and petri dishes in another, warmer laboratory.

She opened the box before her, lifting out a stack of books.

"So many new books?" I asked, in a tone harsher than intended.

"Not new. These are the only ones I did not burn." She handed me one whose location she seemed to remember exactly.

I accepted it, taking note only that it was

worn, not registering what it was, relieved that she would speak to me. "You go to Georgia then," I said.

I pictured her there, in the cornucopia of the Union, surrounded by hanging pomegranates ripened to a red-orange color like no other. I saw her mouth stained a pale but fresh and purpling red, not the color of blood, from their seeds. She was dipping flat bread into a rich walnut paste and spooning potato soup, scented with fresh dill, between her lips. She was wearing her necklace of dried beans from the New World, and it lifted slightly as she swallowed.

Though I said none of this aloud, she nodded and smiled broadly.

—

More than half a million victims of the blockade are buried in the expansive Piskariovskoye Memorial Garden. More than half a million, mostly civilians. These bones that were people are gulped by mass graves — 186 slightly raised mounds that conceal so much.

The bronze figure of a woman, symbol of the mother country, leans toward them, hips rounded, grieving but herself ample.

—

Though I took the last of no variety of the institute's collections, many are now gone. In the absence of money, and, in certain years, interest, some of Lidia's rainbow of legumes, some of the rare landraces of rice that Alena used for her breeding program, were lost to improper storage. What we saved from rats and cold during the winter of hunger fell to rats and heat and humidity in less meager times. Some varieties that needed to be grown out and re-collected every four or five years were left unsowed for decades, as the scientists who cared about them begged money from international conferences and foundations.

A building cannot save what belongs to the fields and gardens of living people.

—

Voltaire got it right in *Candide*, I believe: a bit of decency and the physical labor and small rewards of cultivating a garden from seed are the best we can strive or hope for to dull the pain of lost expectation, or to cover our vices of weakness, boredom, and need.

But I've always preferred the endings of his earlier works, when he still believed that we could find sense in suffering and make meaning through history. I prefer the image of Zadig, married to his beautiful and virtuous (if somewhat dull) wife and crowned king of a Babylon of peace, glory, and abundance. "Men blessed Zadig, and Zadig blessed heaven."

But unlike Zadig, we do not inhabit a world guided by Providence. Ours is a world with only apparent design.

Even in *Candide*, Voltaire was an optimist.

—

The Komarov Institute, where Alena had refused to ask for a job because it housed so many of the great director's libelers, lost twenty-four of its twenty-five greenhouses to Hitlerite bombs and shells.

I knew that this would not have pleased Alena, who would have valued the lost tropical and subtropical collections so much more than she could value revenge. She would have felt relief that at least the building that housed the herbarium and library was not hit, sparing the books. She was a woman who cared more about what she was right about than about being right. That I knew about her, though I could not claim to understand her. Even now, I cannot claim to have understood her.

—

Though early in the hunger winter thieves had dug up their flower bulbs to boil into soup, the

Botanical Gardens had fared much better than the Komarov Institute.

Later in the war, tanks pursued by German aircraft tried to hide under the Gardens' fine trees. But when it was explained to the commander that he would bring destruction in moments to what had been cultivated for two hundred years, he ordered his men to keep moving.

How they fared depends on who is telling the story, but the most reliable sources say they escaped Hitlerite air fire on that day. I do not know which ending makes the better story, which makes the commander the more heroic figure.

The Gardens held their jubilee in February on an evening following one of our rare cloudless days, a day glorious and glinting with hard edges.

I slipped away from watercress tidbits, sliced cheeses, smoked fish, and pickled miniature beets, away from the people, wearing their new shirts and viewing books of flowers that were pressed into thick blue paper by queens two generations and millions of births and deaths earlier.

Almost alone in the fecund greenhouse, greenhouse number twenty-two, alone except for one other man, tall like me, alone like me, eluding greeting like me.

Banana trees pushed at the glass ceiling, fronds of palm and fern brushed my face, and I breathed in the smell of damp soil and violets. I avoided the other man, who stood before the date palms in some possible tribute to nourishment.

I bypassed the whites and pinks and fabulous reds of flowers, the benevolent ignorance of green foliage, and found myself before the cacti, identifying the exact specimens, grown some-what larger now, that Alena had wiped with her nimble hands, risking her delicate skin to their spines.

I imagined her fingers on the last day I could remember her wiping the cacti. Not the last day that she had done so, but the last time I could remember in its particulars and certainly one of her last days.

And I remembered her hands, stained pink with beet juice, on the afternoon she was taken from our flat, and conjured them preparing glass slides for the microscope in the neat movements of well-known but loved work.

And finally I invoked them as I most wanted them to be, soft and held between my own hands, large and undeserving.

In each memory, her hands were small and pretty-boned, the fine pink nails groomed very short and yet still more elegant than the nails that Lidia had always grown long and shaped with pumice – nails that had left scratches on my back to hide from my wife, who either never saw them or never asked.

—

The week following the jubilee, I came across the book that Lidia had handed to me before she left the institute, and at last looked at it. Written by Mikhail Osipovich Gershenzon, it had been published in Moscow back in 1917. The red cloth cover was dirty and badly frayed, but inside, the pages had stayed remarkably close to white.

A passage had been underlined, perhaps by Lidia, perhaps by an earlier hand. It clung to me: "Centuries will pass; faith will again be made simple and personal. Work will be joyful, personal creativity; ownership, an intimate contact with a thing. But faith, work, and ownership will be immutable and holy in the person, enormously enriched inside, like an ear of corn grown out of a seed."

The next day, I wrote to Albertine's guardians, asking them to hold a letter for her until she was mature. In that letter, on one of the crisp sheets of paper now available throughout the city, I told her about her father's sense of humor and fondness for dogs, about her mother's facile mind and elegant posture. I told her that I had loved Alena and that Alena had loved her and that Alena had died. You were right, I told her, when you said that we would never again see them here. I signed my name in a large, clear script.

For years I did not know if my letter had passed through censors and through Europe's ruins. Then one day, at the beginning of late life, shortly after the infernal Lysenko was deemed irrelevant and the great director's name was declared rehabilitated as arbitrarily as he had been named a traitor, I received a letter of thanks from the woman I had known briefly as a small girl. She thanked me for the details about her parents, whom she missed but remembered only as dreamed. She thanked me for arranging her life in France. She said it was an ordinary life raising plump children. She said it was a good life.

—

It was shortly after I wrote my letter to Albertine that I went back to work with purpose, instead of merely inhabiting my small laboratory.

Departing from my earlier studies, I investigated the properties of a fungus that can produce protein from pulp. Through long hours of work I discovered that, if the competitors of this fungus are destroyed with heat, it yields a protein-rich mass.

This dense protein is the sepia color of old photographs, the very color of nostalgia. A kilogram of it can replace three kilograms of meat in a human diet.

These not insignificant findings would save, quite directly, lives at the end of at least two famines.

Even now, on cold days when my stomach growls, I tell myself that I have earned my survival. But on hot nights, when I awake in sweat, I know that redemption, if possible, is irrelevant. A man is ruled by appetite and remorse, and I swallowed what I could.

—

My pantry is full. There are jars filled with different shapes and colors of pasta, with red and brown lentils, with long-and short-grained rice. There are cans of peas, corn, artichokes, mushrooms, white asparagus, and pickled beets. There are cans of pineapple rings and crushed pineapple, cans of peaches, apricots, mandarin oranges, and blackberries. I have, together in a single can, kinds of tropical fruit that are not even grown on the same continent. There are also cans of tuna, salmon, clams, and processed meat. There are boxes of cereal and bouillon cubes. There are packages of raisins and walnuts and almonds and filberts and chocolate candies. I am never without at least several months of provisions.

I reach behind all of this abundance, all of this safety, to a canning jar with a wooden lid. In the jar, I have reproduced each mouthful of food I stole during the winter of hunger. I could not obtain the exact varieties of each kind of seed, of course, but I have put in two tablespoons of a type of teff to represent the teff I ate so secretly in the hallways outside the collection that I was trusted to guard. I have added small handfuls of white Asian rice and nut-scented brown rice from Louisiana, some yellow split peas, seven melon seeds, a few sunflower seeds, a quarter cup of amaranth, three tablespoons of millet, and one mango pit.

Unlike the rainbows of seeds and grains I have seen photographed in catalogs, these look more bland than tempting. Together, they do not fill half the jar.

I wonder if such a meager portion could have kept my Alena alive and what it would be like to know her into old age. It is an unbearably sweet thought for an old man who shares his flat with only nonperishable food.

Shaking these seeds that mean my life, I see that they are beautiful.

Acknowledgments

This novel was not written without help. I drew historical fact and color from the following excellent books: *The 900 Days* by Harrison Evans Salisbury; *Everyday Stalinism* by Sheila Fitzpatrick; *The Vavilov Affair* by Mark Popovsky; *The Lysenko Affair* by David Joravsky; *The Komarov Institute* by Stanwyn Shetler; *Babylon* by Joan Oates; *The Ancient Near East*, edited by James B. Pritchard; *Daily Life in Ancient Mesopotamia* by Karen Rhea Nemet-Nejat; *Everyday life in Babylon and Assyria* by Georges Contenau; and *Leningrad Diary* by Vera Inber, translated by Serge M. Wolff and Rachel Grieve. I also gained information from Web-published material by Barry Mendel Cohen and photographer Ilya Narovlyansky. I got an idea and a reading of Voltaire from Susan Neiman's terrific book *Evil in Modern Thought*. The epigraph from Paul Valéry is from *The Outlook for Intelligence*, translated by Denise Folliot and Jackson Mathews. Throughout the writing, I drew inspiration and information from the publications and important work of the Seed Savers Exchange.

—

I am grateful to everyone at Little, Brown and Company, especially Michael Pietsch and Asya Muchnick. Thanks to John Ware, friend and fabulous agent. I also thank for their crucial support Meredith Blackwell, other members of my family (including Blackwells, Mays, and Bajos), and my friends. I am indebted to the writing program of the University of California, Irvine, the Squaw Valley Community of Writers, and Princeton University Press. For recognizing in me abilities not necessarily apparent to others, Dan Howell, Patricia

Geary, Louis Owens, Paul Majkut, Mary Reardon, and Adam Fortgang deserve special thanks.

Any appreciation I could extend to David Bajo or to Esme Claire Bajo would fall absurdly short. I dedicate this book to them.